The fox and chicken-to-go

Story by Beverley Randell
Illustrations by Rachel Tonkin

A mother fox
lived under a garden shed.

She had three little babies.

The mother fox
had to look after her babies
all the time.

The father fox
had to find food for her.
One night
he went down the road
to find a chicken to eat.

The father fox
saw a chicken house in a backyard.

He walked around and around
the chicken house,
looking for a way in.

The fox jumped
up at the door,
but it stayed shut.

"I can't get inside
the chicken house," he said,
and he went on down the road.

Some cars came down the road very fast.

The fox stopped and looked.

The road was not a safe place.

Then the cars stopped
at the red light.
Now it was safe for him
to cross the road.

“I can smell chicken,” said the fox.
“The smell is coming
from Chicken-to-go.”

He saw some big black bags
outside the shop.
He put his nose inside one. **Yes!**

There was a lot of chicken in the bag.

Chicken-to-go

Then a big truck stopped
outside Chicken-to-go.

A man jumped down
and came to get the black bags.

The fox had to run away!

But he was very lucky.

He did have some chicken!

He ran all the way home.

And all the foxes
had chicken-to-go
to eat that night.